Piano Pieces for the Adult Student

ISBN: 0-8256-2004-X

Piano Pieces for the Adult Student

CONTENTS CLASSIFIED BY COMPOSERS

Piano Pieces for the Adult Student

CLASSIFIED INDEX TO CONTENTS

ELEMENTARY

INTERMEDIATE

ADVANCED

FOREWORD *The adult piano student requires material that is basically different than that which is provided the young beginner. Arrangements as well as their fingerings must be suitable, whereas the material itself can be more encompassing both to style and period.*

Yet, the book we have provided is based on the premise that it must last for years and is to be handed down to the young pianist when he too reaches the adult student level.

Only a person with Maxwell Eckstein's background and experience could have provided the research needed to fill these requirements. We know that you will find the material contained herein lives up to our hopes and yours too.

THE PUBLISHER

Anitra's Dance
from Peer Gynt Suite No. I

EDVARD GRIEG,
(1843 - 1907)

Largo

G. F. HÄNDEL
(1685-1759)

Gavotte in D

FRANCOIS JOSEPH GOSSEC
(1734 - 1829)

Poco allegro ma non troppo

Turkish March
(from "the Ruins of Athens")

L. VAN BEETHOVEN
(1770-1827)

Allegretto

La Paloma
(THE DOVE)

CH. DE YRADIER
(1809 - 1865)

15

Dark Eyes

Russian Folk Melody

Joyous Farmer
(HAPPY FARMER)

R. SCHUMANN
(1810-1856)

Allegro (*animato*)

Avalanche

S. HELLER
(1815-1888)

Allegro vivace

Peasant Dance

FRIEDRICH BAUMFELDER, Op. 208, No. 5
(1836 - 1916)

Made in U.S.A.

Soldiers' March

ROB. SCHUMANN
(1810-1856)

Two Guitars

Russian Folk Song

Moderato

Waltz in E Flat

P. TSCHAIKOWSKY
(1840-1893)

Allegro moderato

Menuet

I. J. PADEREWSKI, Op.14, No.1
(1860 - 1941)

Londonderry Air

Irish Melody

Made in U.S.A.

Fuer Elise
(ALBUMBLATT)

L. VAN BEETHOVEN
(1770-1827)

To Countess Giulietta Guicciardi

First Movement
of the
Sonata quasi una Fantasia
(MOONLIGHT SONATA)

LUDWIG van BEETHOVEN
Op. 27, No. 2

* The highest part requires a firmer touch than the accompanying figure; and the first note in the latter must never produce the effect of a doubling of the melody an octave lower.

Prelude
(Op. 28, No. 7)

FR. CHOPIN
(1810-1849)

à *Madame Camilla Pleyel*

Nocturne

F. CHOPIN, Op. 9, No. 2

Prelude
(Op. 28, No. 20)

FR. CHOPIN

Made in U.S.A.

Serenata

M. MOSZKOWSKI,
(1854 - 1925)

Made in U.S.A.

Guitarre

MORITZ MOSZKOWSKI,
Op. 45, No. 2

Mélodie

M. MOSZKOWSKI,
Op. 18, No. 1

Moderato

Made in U.S.A.

Barcarolle
(TALES OF HOFFMAN)

J. OFFENBACH
(1819-1880)

Moderato

Spinning Song

ALBERT ELLMENREICH

Moment Musical

F. SCHUBERT
(1797-1828)

Sarabande

GEORGE FREDERIC HANDEL
(1685 - 1759)

Made in U.S.A.

On The Meadow

H. LICHNER, Op. 95, No. 2
(1829-1898)

Moderato

The Fountain

Allegretto

C. BOHM, Op. 221
(1844-1920)

Minuet in G

L. VAN BEETHOVEN
(1770-1827)

Allegretto (ma non troppo)

r.h. alone for phrasing

D.S. % al Fine

Bourrée

G. F. HANDEL

Allegro

Bourrée. An old French Dance in quick tempo dating from about 1580. In style and construction similar to the Gavotte, but beginning on the last beat of a measure.

Made in U.S.A.

Romanze
(Op. 68, No. 19)

R. SCHUMANN
(1810-1856)

Valse Lente
(From the Ballet "Coppélia")

LEO. DELIBES
(1836-1891)

Tempo di Valse

Made in U.S.A.

Träumerei

R. SCHUMANN
(1810-1856)

Made in U.S.A.

Waltz Of The Flowers
(From the Nutcracker Suite)

P. TSCHAIKOWSKY
(1840-1893)

Venetian Boat Song
NO. 2

F. MENDELSSOHN, Op. 30, No. 6
(1809-1847)

Allegretto tranquillo

Made in U.S.A.

Valse Bleue

ALFRED MARGIS

Made in U.S.A.

TRIO

ben cantando

mf

Fine

Serenade

F. SCHUBERT
(1797-1828)

Ped. simile

Made in U.S.A

Merry Widow Waltz

F. LEHÁR
(1870 - 1948)

Tempo di Valse *Molto e tranquillo*

Made in U.S.A.

Spring Song

Allegretto grazioso

F. MENDELSSOHN
Op. 62, No. 6

Made in U. S. A.

Largo

From the "New World Symphony"

ANTONIN DVOŘÁK
(1841 - 1904)

Made in U.S.A.

96

Tempo I° (Largo ♩= 52)

Scarf-Dance

C. CHAMINADE
(1861 - 1944)

 Made in U.S.A.

Three American Folk Songs

STEPHEN FOSTER
(1826-1864)

I. Swanee River

II. Kentucky Home

III. Old Black Joe

Song Of India

N. RIMSKY- KORSAKOV
(1844-1908)

Prelude
(No. 1, from Well-tempered Clavichord)

J. S. BACH
(1685-1750)

Le Coucou
RONDO

CLAUDE DAQUIN
(1694-1772)

Made in U.S.A.

Elegie
MELODIE

JULES MASSENET, Op. 10
(1842-1912)

Lento, ma non troppo

(con espressione)

animato

Aragonaise
(LE CID)

J. MASSENET
(1842-1912)

Humoreske

ANT. DVOŘÁK, Op. 101, No. 7
(1841-1904)

Poco lento e grazioso (♩ = 72)

Made in U.S.A.

Chaconne

AUGUSTE DURAND
(1830-1909)

Allegretto

Waltzing Doll
(POUPÉE VALSANTE)

ED. POLDINI
(1869 - 1957)

Tempo di Valse

Le Tambourin

JEAN- PHILIPPE RAMEAU
(1683 - 1764)

Gipsy Rondo
(HUNGARIAN RONDO)

Presto
sempre scherzando

JOSEF HAYDN
(1732 - 1809)

Made in U.S.A.

Minore I

Maggiore

Minore II

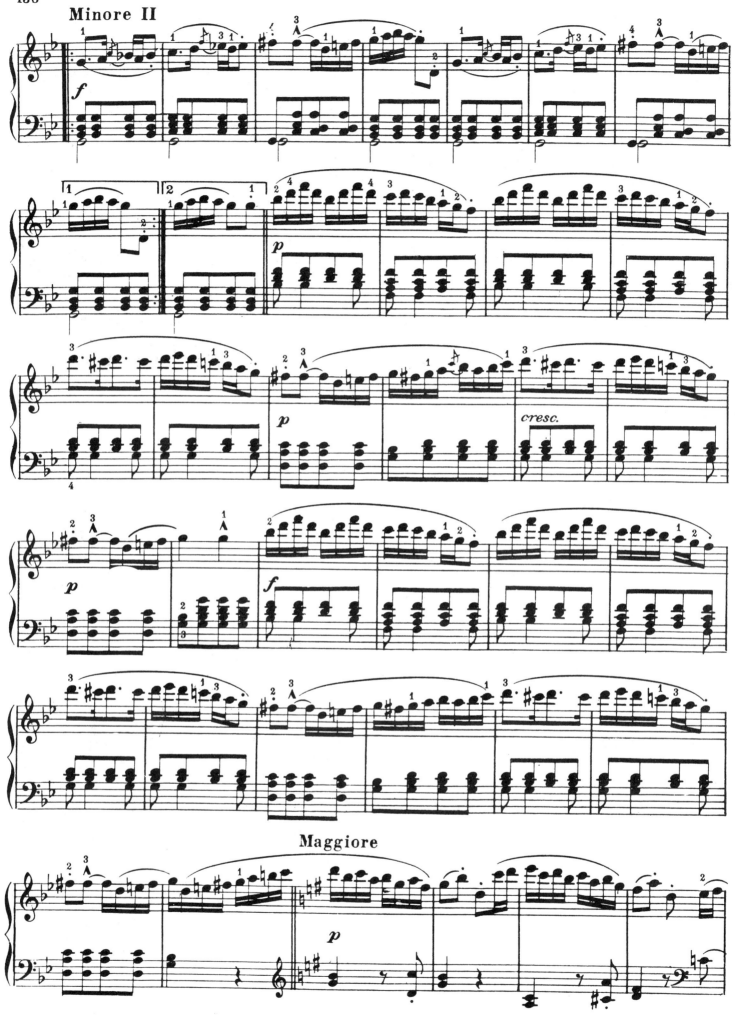

A Madame la Comtesse Delphine Potocka

Valse

F. CHOPIN
Op.64, No.1

Molto vivace

Made in U.S.A

Hungarian Dance
No. 5

JOHANNES BRAHMS
(1833 - 1897)

Allegro

Made in U.S.A.

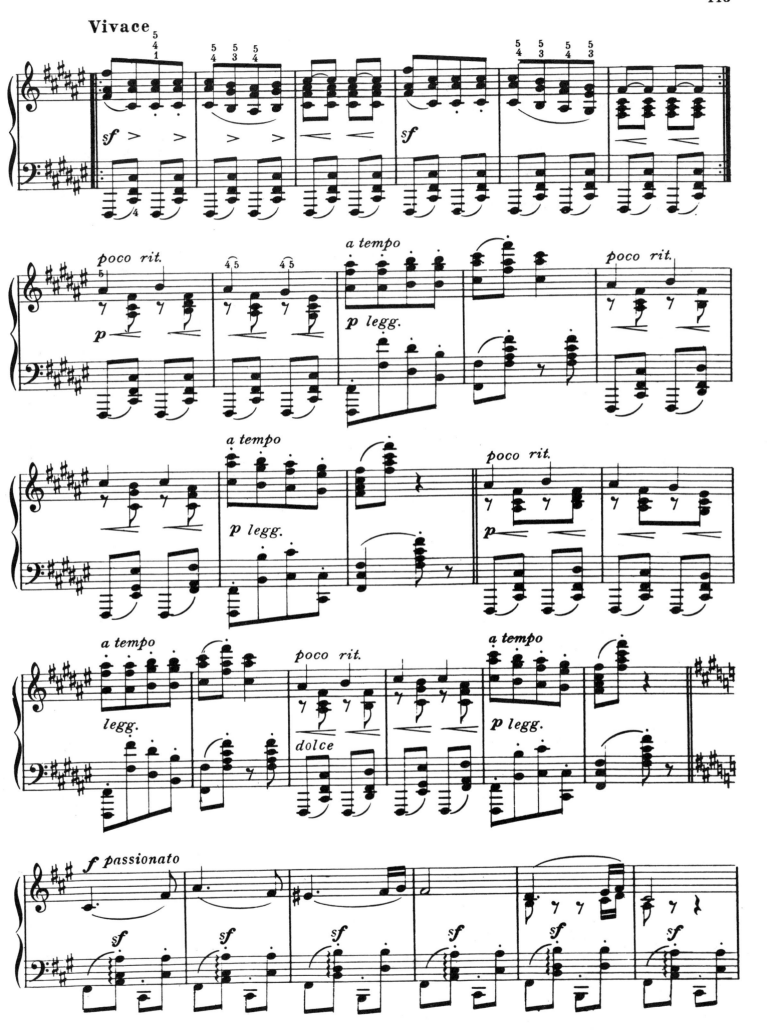

June
BARCAROLLE

P. TSCHAIKOWSKY,
Op. 37, No. 6

Andante cantabile

Made in U.S.A.

Poco più mosso

Andante cantabile
Tempo I

À Madame Nathaniel de Rothschild

Valse

F. CHOPIN
Op. 64, No.2

Made in U.S.A.

Più mosso

Tempo I

Più mosso

Le Secret
INTERMEZZO PIZZICATO

LÉONARD GAUTIER

Made in U.S.A.

March Militaire

FRANZ SCHUBERT
(1797 - 1828)

TRIO

Marcia D.C.

Chanson Triste

Allegro non troppo
con molta espressione

P. TSCHAIKOWSKY,
Op. 40, No. 2

Made in U.S.A.

Minuet
(DON JUAN)

W. A. MOZART
(1756-1791)

Moderato

p

Fine

f

poco rit.

D.C.

Made in U.S.A.

Romance

A. RUBINSTEIN, Op. 44

Andante con moto

p

Made in U.S.A

Mélodie
(MELODY IN F)

A. RUBINSTEIN, Op. 3
(1829 - 1894)

The melody is to be played only with the thumb.

Moderato

Made in U.S.A.

170

Ecossaises

L. VAN BEETHOVEN - BUSONI

Leggero ed animato

5th Nocturne

J. LEYBACH

Flower Song

G. LANGE, Op. 39

Made in U.S.A.

187

Polish Dance
1.

XAVER SCHARWENKA
(1850 - 1924)